LEAD THE FIELD

By Earl Nightingale

Lesson 1:

The Magic Word

&

Acres of Diamonds

All rights reserved. No part of this publication may be reproduced, stored in a retrieval system, or transmitted in any form or by any means, electronic, mechanical, photocopying or otherwise, without the prior permission of the copyright owner.

This book is a transcription of the original
Recording of: LEAD THE FIELD

© Copyright 2006 – BN Publishing

www.bnpublishing.com

info@bnpublishing.com

Transcription: Deena W.

ALL RIGHTS RESERVED

Printed in the U.S.A.

Intoduction

When was the last time something really excited you? Excited you so much, that you couldn't wait to share it with others? Often, such a reaction can be triggered by the simplest and most obvious things - like a tiny puppy, or falling in love, or renewing an old friendship. The great ideas in "Lead the Field" can have that affect on us too. They can turn our lives upside down. Suddenly, the lights are turned on and we can see the world much more clearly. Opportunities take on new luster, even though they have been there all the time. Unnoticed, waiting for the great idea to make them glow.

The multi-faceted career of Earl Nightingale, author and narrator of "Lead the Field", is an affirmation of the affect of great ideas on our lives, and the degree of success we attain. As a teenager, Earl saw the plight of his family and friends in the worst of the Depression. At that time, he couldn't afford any books. So he began seeking the answers, the keys to a better life, in his local library. And as a voracious reader, he kept searching the rest of his life.

After serving as a U.S. marine in World War II, Earl became a well-known broadcast personality and was inducted into the Radio Hall of Fame, where his many achievements as an entrepreneur, writer, public speaker, recording artist and radio and television commentator, he also won a gold record for the LP "The Strangest Secret" for sales exceeding a million copies; the Golden Gavel award from Toastmasters International; the Napoleon Hill Foundation Gold Medal Award for literary excellence; and was inducted into the International Speakers Hall of Fame. He authored numerous audio and video programs, more than 7,000 radio and television commentaries, and two best-selling books.

In "Lead the Field", Earl Nightingale will lead you down new paths and old familiar trails. You'll rediscover the power of words like "attitude" and "service" and "goals" and "commitment". You'll learn the use of "intelligent objectivity", and the benefit of being "constructively discontented", and with each repeated listening you'll unearth new gems from these "acres of diamonds".

Hundreds of thousands of men and women have benefited over the years from this treasury of great ideas and sound. "Lead the Field" is the synthesis of a lifetime of research, reading and refining by Earl

Nightingale. Starting with your first session, "The Magic Word", the messages you're about to hear are widely considered all-time classics in the field of personal development.

This is Earl Nightingale edition of "Lead the Field". This program is about 12 ideas that will bring order and success into our lives. These ideas will work wonders regardless of what we choose as the main thrust of our lives, for these are the great ideas that have evolved over the centuries, and together they form a constellation by which you and I can safely and successfully navigate.

The great Spanish philosopher Ortega reminded us that we human beings are the only creatures on the planet Earth that are born into a natural state of disorientation with our world. That is, while all other creatures are guided by instinct of which they're neither aware nor have the capacity to question, each of us as human creatures was given the

God like power to create his or her own life, and each of us does exactly that all the years of his or her life. Everyday we put in place actions and ideas that will determine the shape and substance of our tomorrows.

For some, those ideas and actions lead inevitably to extraordinary achievement and rewards. For most, they tend to lead to a kind of middle-ground in which great numbers of people take their cues from each other, without question or consideration; and for some, those actions and ideas lead to repeated frustration and problems as they spend their lives in the bottom layers of the socioeconomic pyramid.

Success or failure as a human being is not a matter of luck, or circumstance, or fate, or of breaks, or 'who-you-know', or any of the other tiresome, old myths and clichés by which the ignorant tend to excuse themselves. It's a matter of following a common sense paradigm of rules; guidelines anyone can follow.

Now this program "Lead the Field", has changed more lives, brought about more success stories, helped create more millionaires, saved more careers, important jobs and marriages than any other program ever produced. And the rules we talk about here don't change. They apply to any situation, under any and all circumstances. We never have to say, "I wonder what'll work in this particular situation." All we have to do is make these ideas our own, and we begin with what I call: "The Magic Word".

The Magic Word

We all want good results from life - in our home, our work, and in all our contacts with other people; and the most important single factor to guarantee good results day-in, day-out, all the months and years of our lives, is a healthy attitude.

Attitude is the Magic Word. Attitude is defined as: "The position or bearing as indicating action, feeling or mood", and it is our actions, feeling or moods which determine the actions, feelings and moods of others. Our attitude tells the world what we expect in return. If it's a cheerful, expectant attitude, it says to everyone with whom we come in contact that we expect the best in our dealings with our world. You see, we tend to live up to our expectations, and others give to us as far as their attitudes are concerned - what we expect.

Our attitude is something we can control. We can establish our attitude each morning when we start our day; in fact, we do just that whether we realize it or not. And the people in our family, all the people in our world, will reflect back to us the attitude we present to them. It is then our attitude toward life which determines life's attitude toward us. Cause - and effect. Everything we say or do will cause a corresponding effect. If we're cheerful, glad to be experiencing this miracle of life, others will reflect that good cheer back to us. We are the kind of person others enjoy being around.

You and I are responsible for our lives. You and I produce causes all day long, everyday of our lives. The environment can only return to us a corresponding effect. That's why I say each of us determines the quality of her or his own life. We get back what we put out.

Now here's a way to test the past quality of your attitude. Would you say people tend to react to you with a smiling, positive manner, with friendly greetings when you appear? Your answer to that question will tell the story.

I remember a time when a man and his wife bought a home across the street from me in Florida. They had moved there from Minnesota. They had planned to move for years. They were tired of the Northern winters and he was an avid fisherman. Several months past after their move and one day I was surprised to see them packing. I walked across the street and asked the man if they were leaving so soon after they made the move. He nodded. "My wife hates it here", he said. "We're going back home." I asked him how in the world his wife could hate it there, what his wife didn't like about the place; and with a few questions, the truth came out.

"She hasn't been accepted here", he said. "The other women in the community have left her strictly alone. She's made no friends, she hasn't been asked to participate in any of the community activities." So I asked him, "Has she let the other women know she's interested in participating in community activities?" He stopped what he was doing and looked at me. "No", he said, "No, she hasn't. She's been waiting for the women to ask her."

And since she stayed in the house, waiting for them to come to her, they thought of her as reclusive, as a person who's not interested in making friends, so they've left her alone.

Well, there was a long silence and he began nodding. "Yes, that's exactly what's happened", he said.

Yes, the women of the neighborhood should have come to her and introduced themselves or invited her to a tea or luncheon, but they were reacting to her. She didn't know that the community could only give her back a reflection of her own attitude. Here was a woman in her sixties who had never learned the first important rule for successful living: that our surroundings will always reflect us; that our environment is a mirror – often a merciless mirror – of ourselves.

As soon as a person begins to change, his or her surroundings will change, and it works like this: Great attitude – great results. Good attitude – good results. Fair or average attitude – fair or average results. Poor attitude – poor results. So each of us shapes his or her own life, and to an altogether unexpected extent, the shape and texture, the quality or the lack of quality of our lives is determined by our habitual attitude. Now it sounds simple, doesn't it? But it's not quite that easy. For most of us, learning this new habit takes time. But once it becomes a habit-knit part of our lives, our world will change as dramatically as would walking from a dark cave into the bright light of day.

Most people never think about their attitudes at all; for most of them it's a matter of beginning each day in neutral. Their attitudes are neither good nor bad, but are poised to react to whatever stimuli they encounter. If the stimulus is good, they'll reflect it. If it's bad, they'll reflect that too. They're chameleons, and they go through their days reacting to whatever confronts them - and these are the people of our environment.

That's why it's so important for us to control OUR attitudes, to make sure they're excellent or good.

A person with a poor attitude toward learning, for example, isn't going to learn very much. I know you can think of examples of this in your own life. If we take the attitude that we can't do something, we generally will not do it. An attitude of failure, and we're whipped before we start.

It was William James of Harvard, the founder of psychology in America who said, "Human beings can alter their lives by altering their attitudes of mind". In trying to describe the attitude that's worked so well for me over the years, I found myself using two important words: "gratitude" and "expectant".

First, I'm grateful for the opportunity to live on this beautiful and astonishing planet Earth. I wake up with a sense of gratitude in the morning. Secondly, I expect the best. I expect to reach the goals I establish for myself, about which we'll talk a good deal more later in the program. I find the idea of fulfilling those goals agreeable; hence, the attitude of expectancy. I know the world will give me back what I put out in the way of attitude, so it's up to me. I'm responsible.

There are millions of human beings living their old, dark and frustrated lives, living defensively, simply because they take a defensive, doubtful attitude toward themselves, and as a result toward life in general. A person with a poor attitude becomes a magnet for unpleasant experiences. When those experiences come, as they must because of these attitudes, they tend to reinforce this poor attitude, thereby bringing more problems and so on. The person becomes an example of self-generating, doom-fulfilling prophecy, and it's all a matter, believe it or not – of attitude. We get what we expect, and our outlook on life is a kind of paintbrush, and with it we paint our world. It can be bright and filled with hope and satisfaction, or it can be dark and gloomy. LEGUGLIOUS

It's hard to convince people sometimes that the world they experience is a reflection of their attitude. They take the attitude that if people would only be nice to them, they'd be nice in return. They're like the person who's sitting in front of a cold stove - waiting for the heat. Until they put in the fuel, there's not going to be any heat. It's up to them to act first. It has to start somewhere: Let it begin with us.

Attitude is a reflection of a person inside. Consider for a moment the people who go sailing through life from one success to another, and who, when they occasionally fail at something, shrug it off and head right out again. No matter what a person does, wherever you find a person doing an outstanding job and getting outstanding results, you'll find a person with a good attitude. These people take the attitude toward themselves that they CAN accomplish what they set out to accomplish. They take the attitude that achievement is the natural order of things – and it is! That there's no good reason on earth why they can't be as successful, as competent as anyone else. They have a healthy attitude toward themselves and as a result toward life and the things they want to accomplish. And because of that, they accomplish some remarkable things, in company called 'successful' and 'outstanding' and 'brilliant' and 'lucky', and so on. They're quite frequently no smarter or more talented than most other people, but they have the right attitude. They find their accomplishments not too difficult, simply because it seems so few others are really trying, or really believe in themselves.

As for luck, forget it. Luck is what happens when preparedness meets opportunity, and opportunity is there all the time.

A person can be very efficient at his or her work, but if the corresponding excellent attitude isn't present, well – the person's a failure. A robot can do a great job, but only a human being can ennoble work with a great attitude - and by so doing touch it with the magic of humanness, make it come alive and sing, make it truly worthwhile. That, my friend, makes the difference.

Successful people come in all sizes, shapes, ages and colors, and in widely varying degrees of intelligence and education. But they have one thing in common: They expect more good out of life than bad. They expect to succeed more often than they fail, and they do.

Now there are things you want – worthwhile things. Take the attitude that there are a lot more reasons why you CAN reach those goals than fear of any attempt. Go after them! Work at it. Keep your attitude positive, cheerful and expectant, and you'll get them. And as you do you'll grow to new plateaus and be able to accomplish still more. And remember this: Our environment, the world in which we find ourselves living and working, is a mirror of our attitudes and expectations. If we feel that our environment could stand some improvement, we can bring about that change for the better by improving our attitude. The world plays no favorites; it's impersonal. It doesn't care who succeeds or who fails, nor does it care if we change. Our attitude toward life doesn't affect the world and the people in it nearly so much as it affects us.

It would be impossible to even estimate the number of jobs that have been lost, promotions or good grades missed, sales lost or marriages ruined, by poor attitudes. But you can number in the millions the jobs which are held but hated, the marriages which are tolerated but unhappy, the parents and children who fail to understand and love one another, all because of people who are waiting for the world and others to change toward them. They don't understand that what they're getting is a reflection of themselves. Nothing can change until we do. When we change, our worlds will change. The answer is attitude.

How does one develop a good attitude? The same way one develops any other factor: Practice. One good way is to stick a small sign on the bathroom mirror on which is printed the word "attitude". That way you'll see it first thing every morning. You might have another one in your car and at your place of work - - we need to smile more, speak to people, go out to people. Everything in the world we want to do and get done we must do with and through people. Every dollar we will ever earn must come from people. Everything worthwhile, the person we love and with whom we want to spend the rest of our life, is a human being with whom we must interact. Our children are individuals, each different from any other person who ever lived. And what affects them most is our attitude - the loving kindness they see and feel whenever we're around.

If you begin to develop a golden attitude that says "YES" to life and the world, you'll be astonished at the changes you'll see. Someone once said, "Life is dull." Only to dull people – it's true. Of course, it's also true that life is interesting only to interesting people, and life is successful only for successful people. We must be the epitome, the embodiment. We must radiate success before it'll come to us. We must first become mentally - from an attitude standpoint - the people we wish to become.

Many years ago, a famous Los Angeles restauranteur was asked by a newspaper reporter, "When did you become successful?" And he replied: "I was successful when I was dead broke. I knew what I wanted to do, and I knew I'd do it. It was only a matter of time." He had a successful attitude long before the success he sought had become a reality. The great German philosopher and writer, Gerta, put it this way: "Before you can do something, you must be something."

But let me prove my point by giving you a test. If you will conscientiously go about the test I'll outline and concentrate on it every day, you'll find yourself becoming 'lucky', as the uninitiated call it; all sorts of wonderful things will begin happening in your life and it will show you what a great attitude can mean.

So here's the test: Treat every person with whom you come in contact as the most important person on earth.

Now you do that for three excellent reasons: One, as far as every person is concerned, he or she IS the most important person on earth. Two, because that's the way human beings ought to treat each other. And Three, by treating everyone this way, we begin to form an important habit. There's nothing in the world that men, women and children want and need more than self-esteem: The feeling that they're important, that they're recognized, that they're needed, that they count and are respected. They will give their love, their respect and their business to the person who fills this need, even if it's a short encounter.

Have you ever noticed that the higher you go in any organization of value, the nicer the people seem to become? It works this way: The bigger the people, the easier it is to talk to them, to get on with them, and work with them. So they naturally matriculate to the top. It's their attitudes. And the people with great attitudes just naturally gravitate to the top of whatever business or department they're in. They don't have great attitudes because of their positions; they have their positions largely because of their great attitudes.

For the purposes of this test, act toward others in exactly the same manner that you want them to act toward you. Treat the members of your family as the very important people they really are – the most important in the world. Carry out into the world each morning the kind of attitude you'd have if you were the most successful person on earth. Notice how quickly it develops into a habit. For almost immediately a change will be noticed. Irritations that used to frustrate you begin to disappear. When some less informed person gives you a bad time, don't let his poor attitude infect yours. Keep yours in hand, keep it good, keep cool, above it all, and smiling. If someone cuts in front of your car, or acts in any other manner that shows a lack of courtesy, don't react as he would. Smile it off!

Destructive emotions such as anger, hatred, or jealousy don't hurt others; they hurt you. They can make your life miserable – they can make you sick. Forgive everyone who ever hurt you, really forgive them. And then forgive yourself. That's all past. Stewing over it, exhuming it, can only make you sick. Forgive and forget it. Get rid of it. You've risen above that sort of thing.

And as you develop a great attitude, you'll probably realize that you've already placed yourself on the road to what you seek. You're well on your way. It makes no difference how successful you may have been in the past - you'll be delighted with the ease and comfort of your new life.

The bad or poor attitudes of others can be as infectious as the common cold. It's important that we look on them in this light: As infectious conditions that can only end by hurting and annoying us if we allow ourselves to catch them. Art the doctor? Often working with people with infectious conditions? We must keep ourselves healthy, we simply don't have time for that sort of thing.

Whoever started the cliché, "Life's too short", certainly knew what he or she was talking about. It really is too short, much too short to spend any of our valuable time mimicking the attitudes of others – unless they're good! A great attitude does much more than turn on the lights in our world. It seems to magically connect us to all sorts of serendipitous opportunities that were somehow absent before the change. Maybe that's what people mean when they say we're 'lucky'. Suddenly we do find ourselves getting the so-called 'breaks', but it's really nothing more than this new connection with the world that comes with a great attitude. We find ourselves doing more, and doing it in less time. We put ourselves directly in the path of all kinds of serendipitous happenings.

When you begin to develop a better attitude you'll realize that you've already place yourself in the top five percent of the people – the most successful people on earth. You've placed yourself on the road to what you seek. You've prepared the ground, you've only to plant the seed.

Now in summing up, here are a few points to keep in mind:

First, it's our attitude at the beginning of a difficult task which more than anything else will bring about its successful outcome.

Secondly, our attitudes toward others determine their attitudes toward us. We're all interdependent. The success we achieve in life will depend largely on how well we relate to others.

Thirdly, before you can achieve the kind of life you want, you must think, act, talk, and conduct yourself in all of your affairs, as would the person you wish to become. Keep a mental picture of that person before you as often as you can during the day.

And fourthly, remember that the higher you go in any organization of value, the better the attitudes you'll find. And that attitudes are not the result of success; success is the result of great attitudes.

And finally, the deepest craving of a human being is for recognition and self-esteem, to be needed, to feel important, to be recognized and appreciated. That includes our loved ones and all the people with whom we come in contact during our days.

To make these important principles a habit-knit part of our lives, here are some suggestions:

Since our minds can hold only one thought at a time, make the thoughts you hold constructive and positive. Look for the best in people and ideas. Be constantly alert for new ideas you can put to use in your life. Don't waste time talking about your problems to people who can't solve them, or your health - unless it's good, or you're talking to your doctor. It won't help you; it cannot help others.

Radiate the attitude of well-being and confidence, the attitude of the person who knows where he or she is going. You'll find all sorts of good things happening to you. And lastly, treat everyone with whom you come in contact as the most important person on earth.

Start this habit, practice it consistently, and you'll do it and benefit from it for the rest of your life.

Thank you.

ACRES OF
DIAMONDS

In the year 1843, a man was born who was to have a profound effect on the lives of millions of people. His name was Russell Herman Conwell. He became a lawyer, then a newspaper editor, and finally a clergyman. It was during his church career that an incident occurred which was to change his life and the lives of countless others.

One day a group of young people came to Dr. Conwell in his church and asked him if he'd be willing to instruct them in college courses. They all wanted a college education, but lacked the money to pay for it. He told them to let him think about it and come back in a few days. After they left, an idea began to form in Dr. Conwell's mind. He asked himself, "Why couldn't there be a fine college for poor, but deserving young people?"

And before very long the idea consumed him. Why not indeed! It was a project worthy of 100% dedication, complete commitment, and almost single-handedly Dr. Conwell raised several million dollars with which he founded "Temple University", today one of the country's leading schools.

He raised the money by giving more than 6,000 lectures all over the country, and in each one of them he told a story called "Acres of

Diamonds". It was a true story, which had affected him very deeply, and it had the same effect on his audiences. The money he needed to build the college came pouring in.

The story was the account of an African farmer who heard tales about other farmers, who had made millions by discovering diamond mines. These tales so excited the farmer that he could hardly wait to sell his farm and go prospecting for diamonds himself. So he sold the farm, and spent the rest of his life wandering the African continent searching unsuccessfully for the 'gleaming gems' which brought such high prices on the markets of the world. Finally, the story goes, worn out and in a fit of despondency, he threw himself into a river and drowned.

Meanwhile, back at the ranch, or farm in this case, the man who had bought his farm happened to be crossing the small stream on the property, when suddenly there was a bright flash of blue and red light through the stream bottom. He bent down, picked up the stone – it was a good-sized stone – and admiring it, later put it on his fireplace mantle as an interesting curiosity.

Several weeks later, a visitor picked up the stone, looked closely at it, hefted it in his hand, and nearly fainted. He asked the farmer if he knew what he'd found. Well, the farmer said no, that he thought it was a piece of crystal. The visitor told him he had found one of the largest diamonds ever discovered.

Well, the farmer had trouble believing that. He told the man that his creek was full of such stones, not as large perhaps as the one on the mantle, but – well, they were sprinkled generously throughout the creek bottom.

Needless to say, the farm the first farmer had sold so that he might find a diamond mine, turned out to be the most productive diamond mine on the entire African continent. The first farmer had owned, free and clear, acres of diamonds; but had sold them for practically nothing in order to look for them elsewhere.

Well, the moral is clear: If the first farmer had only taken the time to study and prepare himself to learn what diamonds looked like in their rough state, and since he had already owned a piece of the African continent, to thoroughly explore the property he had before looking elsewhere, all of his wildest dreams would have come true.

Now the thing about this story that so profoundly affected Dr. Conwell and subsequently millions of others, was the idea that each of us is at this moment, standing in the middle of his or her own acres of diamonds. If we'll only have the wisdom and patience to intelligently and effectively explore the work in which we're now engaged, to explore ourselves, we'll usually find the richest receipt, whether they be financial or intangible, or both! Before we go running off to what we think are greener pastures, let's make sure that our own is not just as green or perhaps even greener.

It's been said that if the other guy's pasture appears to be greener than ours, it's quite possible that it's getting better care. Besides, while we're looking at other pastures, other people are looking at ours.

There are few things more pitiful to my mind than the person who wastes his life running from one thing to another, forever looking for the pot of gold at the end of the rainbow, and never staying with one thing long enough to find it.

No matter what your goal may be, perhaps the road to it can be found in the very thing you're now doing. It wasn't until he was completely paralyzed by polio and forced to reach into the rich resources of his mind, that a courageous farmer got the idea of producing exceptionally good meat products on his farm. From that idea, one of the country's most successful meat packing companies was born. His farm contained acres of diamonds too; he'd just never had to dig for them before.

Your mind is your richest resource. Let it thoroughly explore the possibilities lurking in what you're presently doing before turning to something new. I say that because there were probably good reasons for your having chosen your present work in the beginning. If there weren't, and if you're unhappy in the field you're in, well – then perhaps it's time for some serious exploration.

Dr. Russell Conwell's life is living example of the importance of a willingness to change once one's own pasture has been thoroughly explored. I said that Dr. Conwell began as a lawyer, then later changed to become a newspaper editor, before he finally found his true calling as a clergyman and the founder of a great University.

One of the best examples of a person finding acres of diamonds hiding in his work is Stu Leonard of Connecticut. He began as a dairy route deliveryman. As he worked his rounds, he began to think of all the products connected to the dairy business that his customers really needed. He bought a working dairy with very little down and a lot of hard work, and began building his business around it. Keeping the working dairy intact in the center of his operations, and surrounding it with windows through which his customers could watch the process, he began adding other products. Today his dairy store is the largest in the world, and it sells everything in the food line. People come from all over the entire area to shop at Stu Leonard's dairy store, and they love it - and he loves them.

People who are too old or infirm to come to his store on their own are picked up in Stu Leonard's buses and brought to the store. He has a multi-million dollar business that grew out of a delivery route. The diamonds were there – and Stu Leonard made the most of them.

Every kind of work has such opportunity lurking within it. The opportunities are there now, clamoring to be noticed. But they cannot speak, or print signs for us to read. Our part of the bargain is to look at our work with new eyes, with the eyes of creation.

Tyre Dejardin said: "It is our duty as men and women to proceed, as the limits to our abilities do not exist. We are collaborators in creation."

A man I knew in Arizona began with a small gas station. One day sitting at his desk and watching through the window while one of his young attendants filled a man's gas tank, he watched the customer while he stood about waiting for the job to be finished. It dawned upon him that that man had money in hi pockets, and there were things he needed, or wanted, that he'd pay for if they were conveniently displayed where he could see them. So, he began adding things: fishing tackle, then fishing licenses; hunting and camping equipment; rifles, shotguns, ammunition, hunting licenses. He found an excellent line of aluminum fishing boats and trailers. He began buying up the continuous property around him; then he added an auto parts department. He'd always carried cold soft drinks and candy, but now he added an excellent line of chocolates in a refrigerated case. Before long, he sold more chocolates than anyone else in the state!

He carried thousands of things his customers could buy while waiting for their cars to be serviced. All the products he sold also guaranteed that most of the gas customers in town would come to his station – he sold more gas. He began cashing checks on Friday, and the bonanza grew and grew. It all started with a man with a human brain watching a customer standing around with money in his pockets and nothing to spend it on.

Others would have lived and died with a small service station, and they do. My friend saw the diamonds. Both my friend in Arizona, and Stu Leonard in Connecticut, are customer-oriented. Serve the customer. Serve the customer better than anyone else is serving the customer. Stu Leonard has his company policy conspicuously displayed in his store for all to read, and it goes like this:

Rule Number One: The customer is always right.

Rule Number Two: If you think the customer is wrong, read rule number one again.

Many service station operators, upon seeing a wealthy customer drive in, might say to themselves: "I ought to be in his business". Not so. There's just as much opportunity in one business as another, if we'll only stop playing 'copycat' with each other, and begin to think creatively, begin to think in new directions.

It's there - believe me. And it's our job to find it. Take the time to stand off and look at your work as a stranger might, and ask: "Why does he do it that way? Has he noticed how what he's doing might be capitalized upon, or multiplied?"

If you're happy with things as they are, then by all means, keep them that way. But there's great fun finding diamonds hiding in our selves and in our work. We never get bored or blasé or find ourselves in a rut. A rut, we're reminded, is really nothing more than a grave, with the ends kicked out.

Some of the most interesting businesses in the world grew out of what was originally a very small idea, in a very small area. If something is needed in one town, then the chances are it's also needed in all towns and cities all over the country. You might also ask yourself, "How good am I at what I'm presently doing?" Do you know all there is to know about your work? Would you call yourself a 'first-class professional' at your work? How would your work stand up against the work of others in your line?

The educator and author J. B. Matthews wrote: "Unless a person has trained himself for his chance, the chance will only make him ridiculous. A great occasion is worth to a man exactly what his preparation enables him to make of it." I'm sure Dr. Matthews intended to include the female half of the world in that statement. I'm often appalled by how little people know about the business they're in. "That's not my department", they'll say. I suppose if they see a fire starting in someone else's department, they wouldn't report it.

Most real estate people don't sell homes and property - they show homes and property, something a six-year-old child could do. They often know nothing at all about selling or marketing, yet they call themselves real estate professionals. They're actually tour guides. "This is the living room", they say to intelligent men and women who already know what a living room looks like.

Someone, come to think of it - I think it was me, once wrote that the human race is much like a convoy in time of war. The whole menagerie is slowed down to protect the slowest shifts, and they march on in that dusty valley, unmindful of the diamonds beneath their feet.

The first thing we need to do to become a diamond miner is to break away from the crowd, and quit assuming that because people in the millions are living that way, it must be the best way. It is not the best way! It's the average way. The people going the best way are way out in front. They're so far ahead of the crowd you can't even see their dust anymore. They're the people who live and work on the leading edge, the cutting edge; and they mark the way for all the rest.

We have a choice to make really, you and I. It takes imagination, curious imagination to know that diamonds don't look like cut and polished gem stones in their rough state, nor does a pot of iron ore look like stainless steel. To prospect your own acres of diamonds, develop a faculty we might call "intelligent objectivity". The faculty to stand off and look at your work as a person from Mars might look at it. Within the framework of what industry or profession does your job fall? Do you know all you can about your industry or profession? Is the time for a refreshing change of some kind? How can a customer be given a better break?

Each morning ask yourself, "How can I increase my service today? There are rare and very marketable diamonds lurking all around me. Have I been looking for them, examining every facet of my work and of the industry or profession in which it has its life? There are better ways to do what I'm presently doing. What are they? How will my work be performed 20 years from now? Everything in the world is in a state of evolution and improvement - how can I do what will eventually be done anyway now?"

Think of what Stu Leonard did with his dairy route, and my Arizona friend with his small service station; what famous Amos did with his chocolate chip cookies; what Procter & Gamble did with soap. Sure, there's risk involved - there's no growth of any kind without risk. We start running risks when we get out of bed in the morning. Risks are good for us - they bring out the best that's in us; they brighten the eye and get the mind cooking; they quicken the step and put a new, shining look on our days. Human beings should never be settled. It's OK for chickens and cows and cats, but it's wrong for human beings. People start to die when they become settled. We need to keep things stirred up.

Back in 1931, Lloyd C. Douglas, the world famous novelist who wrote "The Robe", "Magnificent Obsession", and other best-selling books, wrote a magazine article titled "Escape". During that article Douglas asked, "Who of us has not at some time toyed briefly with the temptation to run away? If all the people who have given that idea the temporary hospitality of their imagination were to have acted upon it, few would be living at their present addresses. And that the small minority who did carry the impulse into effect, it's doubtful if many ever disengaged themselves as completely as they had hoped from the problems that hurled them forth. More often than otherwise, it may be surmised, they packed up their troubles in their old kitbags, and took them along."

The point of the article was simply: Don't try to run away from your troubles - overcome them, prevail right where you are. What we're really after is not escape from our perplexities and frustrations, but a triumph over them. And one of the best ways to accomplish that is to get on course and stay there. Restate and reaffirm your goal: the thing you want most to do, the place in life you want most to reach. See it clearly in your mind's eye, just as you can envision the airport in Los Angeles when you board your plane in New York; or like a great ship in a storm - just keep your heady and your engines running. The storm will pass, although sometimes it seems that it never will.

And one bright morning you'll find yourself passing the harbor light. Then you can give a big sigh of relief, rest a while, and almost before you know it, you'll find your eyes turning seaward again. You'll think of a new harbor you'd like to visit, a new voyage upon which to embark. And once again, you'll set out, and that's just the way this funny-looking, two-legged, curious, imaginative, tinkering, fiddling dreamer called a human being operates.

He escaped from problems not by running away from them, but by overcoming them. And no sooner does he overcome one set of problems, but he starts looking around for new and more difficult pickles to get himself into, and out of. So if you find yourself looking at travel folders and thinking of running away, go ahead, think about it. It'll get your mind off things for a while. Then zero in on your goal - more about that later - and get busy.

Take one thing at a time, and before you know it you'll start seeing those diamonds scattered all over your world, and you'll be out in the clear again. If you feel like running away from it all once in a while, you're perfectly normal. If you stay and get rid of your problems by working your way through them, you're a successful citizen.

Start taking an hour a day with a legal pad, and dissect your work. Take it apart and look at its constituent parts. There's opportunity there - that's your acre of diamonds.

We have Book Recommendations for you

The Strangest Secret by Earl Nightingale
(Audio CD - Jan 2006)

The Strangest Secret by Earl Nightingale
(Paperback)

Acres of Diamonds [MP3 AUDIO]
[UNABRIDGED] (Audio CD) by Russell H.
Conwell

Automatic Wealth: The Secrets of the Millionaire
Mind--Including: Acres of Diamonds, As a Man
Thinketh, I Dare you!, The Science of Getting Rich,
The Way to Wealth, and Think and Grow Rich
[UNABRIDGED]
by Napoleon Hill, et al (CD-ROM)

Think and Grow Rich [MP3 AUDIO]
[UNABRIDGED]
by Napoleon Hill, Jason McCoy (Narrator)
(Audio CD - January 30, 2006)

As a Man Thinketh [UNABRIDGED]
by James Allen, Jason McCoy (Narrator) (Audio
CD)

Your Invisible Power: How to Attain Your Desires
by Letting Your Subconscious Mind Work for You
[MP3 AUDIO] [UNABRIDGED]
by Genevieve Behrend, Jason McCoy (Narrator)
(Audio CD)

Thought Vibration or the Law of Attraction in the
Thought World [MP3 AUDIO] [UNABRIDGED]
by William Walker Atkinson, Jason McCoy
(Narrator) (Audio CD - July 1, 2005)

The Law of Success Volume I: The Principles of
Self-Mastery by Napoleon Hill (Audio CD - Feb 21,
2006)

The Law of Success, Volume I: The Principles of
Self-Mastery (Law of Success, Vol 1) (The Law of
Success) by Napoleon Hill (Paperback - Jun 20,
2006)

The Law of Success , Volume II & III: A Definite
Chief Aim & Self Confidence by Napoleon Hill
(Paperback - Jun 20, 2006)

Thought Vibration or the Law of Attraction in the Thought World & Your Invisible Power (Paperback)

Automatic Wealth, The Secrets of the Millionaire Mind-Including: As a Man Thinketh, The Science of Getting Rich, The Way to Wealth and Think and Grow Rich (Paperback)

The Bestsellers on this Book give sound advice about money or how to obtain it. Just shoot to the stars and stay focused on your dreams and it will happen. There is nothing that we can imagine, that we can't do. So what are we waiting for, let's begin the journey of self fullfillment.

4 Bestsellers in 1 Book:

As a Man Thinketh by James Allen

The Science of Getting Rich by Wallace D. Wattles

The Way to Wealth by Benjamin Franklin

Think and Grow Rich by Napoleon Hill

Get Published!

BN Publishing helped authors publish more titles. So whether you're writing a romance novel, historical fiction, mystery, action and suspense, poetry, children's or any other genre, we can help you reach your publishing goals.

Paperback

Reach 20,000 retail accounts in the U.S. (including chains, independents, specialty stories, and libraries).

Including:

www.amazon.com

www.amazon.co.uk

www.amazon.ca

www.bn.com

www.powells.com

www.ebay.com

and more...

Your book will be included in a physical catalog that will go out to over 20,000 retail stores.

When your title is entered into our library it will automatically appear in the bookstore and library databases.

Our United States and United Kingdom based sales teams works with publisher clients based throughout the world who want to print books in the United States and United Kingdom, or reach the North American, UK and wider European markets through our broad distribution channel partners.

If we decide to publish it:

we will send you 2 free copies of the finished book;

we will give you 10% royalty of the selling price of each book copy sold (selling price = the price the book is sold by BN Publishing to wholesalers or other resellers);

and if you wish to have more copies of your book, we will sell you the book for two thirds of the list price.

Please send us more information about your book to info@bnpublishing.com

www.bnpublishing.com

BN Publishing

Improving People's Life

www.bnpublishing.com

BN Publishing

Improving People's Life

www.bnpublishing.com

www.ingramcontent.com/pod-product-compliance
Lightning Source LLC
Chambersburg PA
CBHW032206040426
42449CB00005B/465